I'm a little scientist!

I CAN CHANGE THE WORLD...

T0015146

See a QR code? Scan it to access bonus resources!

Water savers

WITH THE TURN OF A TAP

BY
RONALD CHAN

ILLUSTRATED BY
YEEWEARN

WS Education

NEW JERSEY · LONDON · SINGAPORE · BEIJING · SHANGHAI · HONG KONG · TAIPEI · CHENNAI · TOKYO

It was a lovely Monday morning, the start of a new week of school for Wendy and Sarah.

Wake up, everyone! Time to go to school!

Yes, Dad!

Yes, Dad...

Sarah began her morning routine by brushing her teeth, just like any other day.

But that morning, Wendy happened to glance in. She opened the bathroom door and was horrified by what she saw.

With a sense of urgency, Wendy rushed into the bathroom. She reached out to turn me off, as Sarah looked back at her in confusion.

Wh–t's h–pp–ng–

Sarah rolled her eyes, exasperated. She quickly rinsed her mouth and confronted Wendy.

What's the big fuss, Wendy? It's just a running tap! We've got so much water around us that this isn't going to change anything.

Oh no, Sarah, it's not just a running tap. Water's precious and we've got to save what we can!

"Uh oh, they're starting to argue," I thought to myself. "It's time for me to show myself, and bring them around the world."

Why are we shrinking? Where are we going?

What's happening?!

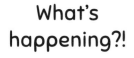

Good morning girls! Wendy's right, I'm not just a running tap, and our water isn't exactly unlimited in supply. With the turn of a tap, you can change the world!

Is that so? How are we going to change the world?

Wait a minute... Who are you?

"My name is Pat the Tap," I said, "and there are many things I want to show you. Let's go, Water Savers!"

Oh dear...

Not to worry, Wendy, you'll be back in time for school. Now, let me first show you where our water comes from.

With that, we swam out towards our water sources.

Let's go, Wendy!
This sounds fun.

Follow me, and you'll
see how we can
change the world!

As we emerged from the pipes into a reservoir, we saw children kayaking and families cycling around.

MEET THE OTTERS

Meet the Bishan Otter Family from Singapore! Otters vanished from Singapore after the 1960s due to water pollution but have recently reappeared after greening initiatives. Keep our water bodies brimming so that animals like the Bishan Otter Family can flourish!

⚠️ Water is transported around Earth through the water cycle. A very small amount of this water (less than 1%!) exists in a fresh and drinkable form. The more water we use up, the harder it is for our reservoirs and lakes to be replenished. Healthy reservoirs and lakes support many recreational activities and safeguard our freshwater supply.

"With the turn of a tap, you can help conserve fresh water," I said. "Did you know that fresh water is precious and limited? Our planet has a lot of water, but most of it isn't drinkable!"

Part of our fresh water comes from the reservoirs and wetlands so saving water helps to keep them full and fun!

Yes, what a lively reservoir! And look at these cute otters!

97% salt water

2.5% fresh water locked up

0.5% accessible fresh water

We soared high above the reservoir and peered down at the world beneath us. "Now, Sarah, tell me what you see!"

Hmm... I see many animals! They look like they're drinking or playing in the water.

MEET HADY,

a hippopotamus who needs to be in water throughout the day to stay cool. It is difficult for Hady to find water during droughts and in places with heavy water usage. Help conserve water so that Hady can stay happy!

Animals need water to stay hydrated, digest their food and keep their bodies cool.

Plants need water for their cell functions and staying cool.

Indeed! With the turn of a tap, we can help preserve wildlife. Animals and plants need fresh water to survive. By conserving water, we leave enough for our animals to keep cool and our plants to stay green!

Rivers are historically cradles of civilisation and are also home to rich biodiversity. Many major cities (indicated by dots) are situated near rivers!

How refreshing! Just what I need for a hot day...

Fresh water is crucial for both people and wildlife. By protecting our wetlands and water bodies from depletion, we keep them healthy and increase our wildlife's chances of survival.

Sneaking into rain clouds, we prepared to take a ride on raindrops back down to Earth. "Your turn, Wendy! What are we looking at?"

MEET RIZAL,

a rice plant grown all around the world and especially in Asia. About a third of the world's fresh water supply dedicated to agriculture is used for rice, as plants like Rizal require a lot of water to grow. It takes about 3000 to 5000 litres of water to produce 1 kilogram of rice!

More than half of the world's fresh water supply goes to farms! This water makes it possible to grow fruits and vegetables, and raise livestock, keeping our food supply stable.

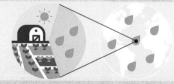

Aha! With the turn of a tap, we can help farms growing crops. A lot of water is needed for rice and wheat!

Yes, by conserving water, we also leave enough water for farms to help these plants to flourish.

In order for homes, farms, cities and wildlife to all have enough clean water, we all have to play our part in responsibly consuming water.

We landed on the ground and headed back towards the pipes. "Great job so far, Water Savers!" I said. "With the turn of a tap, you can also save energy. Look around, and see if you can tell me why!"

I spy... A water pumping station! Energy is needed to move water around.

MEET DANIELA,

a hydroelectric power plant located near a river dam. Daniela uses the potential energy from the water as it falls from a high place to a low place, and turns it into useful electricity. Not all movement of water consumes energy! Water moving downstream can sometimes be made productive by converters like Daniela.

⚠️ Bringing water from rivers and reservoirs to our homes and other places often needs quite a bit of energy!

The more water we use, the more energy we consume. Significant energy usage heats up our planet and drives climate change.

Finally, we entered a labyrinth of pipes beneath a city...

MEET SALLY,

a desalination plant that converts seawater into fresh water. About 97% of Earth's water is in the oceans and too salty for drinking. Desalination plants like Sally remove this salt for us, but they use very specialised equipment and need a lot of energy to operate.

And I spy... Water treatment plants! Energy is needed to clean and treat water too.

⚠ To make sure we have enough fresh water for all, we need effective ways to extract fresh water from the environment, and to clean our used water before returning it to nature.

MEET RENE,

a water treatment plant that converts used water to clean water that can be safely returned to the environment. Some plants go one step further to produce water that is drinkable again! However, they also use very specialised equipment and up to a quarter of the energy used by desalination plants.

Both fresh water extraction and wastewater treatment consume energy. Both processes are expensive!

With that, our mission was accomplished, and the girls had learnt an exciting lesson.

"Well done, Water Savers!" I cheered. "Now it's time to head back home."

Wow, Pat, thanks for showing us so many things! One action has many effects. With the turn of a tap, we can conserve water and change the world!

That's right, girls! Now, off to school you go.

Thanks, Pat!

Bye!

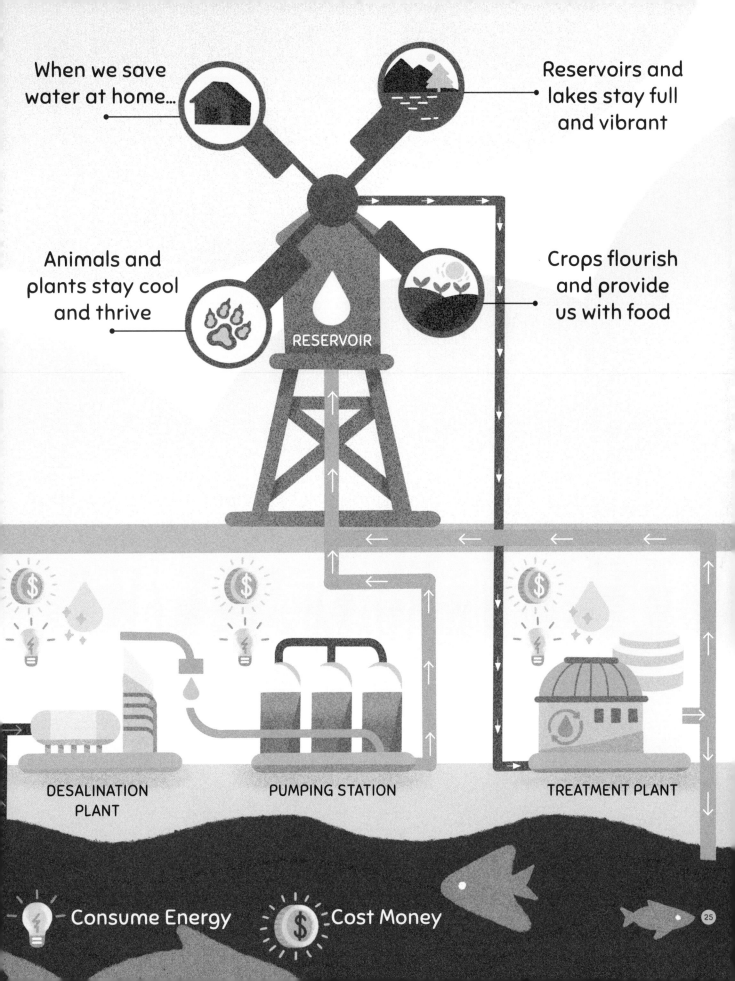

When we save water at home…

Reservoirs and lakes stay full and vibrant

Animals and plants stay cool and thrive

Crops flourish and provide us with food

RESERVOIR

DESALINATION PLANT

PUMPING STATION

TREATMENT PLANT

Consume Energy

Cost Money

And that was enough for one morning! Wendy and Sarah hurried to leave for school.

What took you so long, girls? You're almost late for school!

Don't worry, Dad, we're going to change the world!

Be Water Savers, like Us!

FINDING WATER

Learn more about technological innovations to increase the resilience of our freshwater supply!

WATER CATCHMENT AREAS

Reservoirs and catchment ponds may be used to collect and store rainwater for future use. Some areas also use underground sewers to collect used water for recycling!

salt and other minerals

ultraviolet light

DESALINATION PLANT

By forcing seawater through membranes with tiny holes, desalination plants can remove salt and other minerals (⊖ ⊕) to make the water clean and drinkable.

TREATMENT PLANT

Water treatment plants can also remove harmful organisms and particles from wastewater to produce drinkable water! Ultraviolet light ( ) may be shone on the treated water to further disinfect it.

Several of these technological marvels require the development of materials of novel designs and compositions. See if you can find out more about them!

DID YOU NOTICE?

Did you notice these items in Sarah's and Wendy's bathroom? They can help reduce your consumption of water! See if you have them at home.

Half-flush and full-flush toilets (Pg4): If your home toilet has a half-flush capability, try to use it whenever possible rather than a full flush. Try practising this in mall and school toilets as well. For boys, you might notice that some malls and schools actually have waterless self-cleaning urinals!

Mug for brushing teeth (Pg5): Instead of leaving the tap to run when brushing your teeth, use a mug to hold water for gargling and rinsing your mouth instead. Small changes to your daily lifestyle can make a big difference to water consumption.

Look out for these as well! Here are other ways to make our world more sustainable.

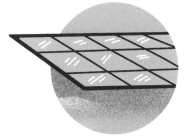

Floating solar panel (Pg15): Solar panels harness the energy of the Sun to generate electricity without greenhouse gas emissions. They have been installed on the surfaces of ponds and reservoirs around the world. These floating panels free up space on land for other uses and also reduce evaporation!

Cattle (Pg18): Livestock can contribute to greenhouse gas emissions. Cattle, for example, generate methane due to their digestive system. Methane actually traps heat in the atmosphere more efficiently than carbon dioxide, and is also a significant contributor to global warming.

Consider plant-based meals and more sustainable meat sources if possible, and try to reduce food wastage!

WHAT CAN I DO AT HOME?

Here are more ways to conserve water at home:

01. Take shorter showers:
Did you know that showering is a key contributor to water usage at home? By taking shorter showers and turning the shower off while you're soaping, you can help to reduce your water usage!

02. Check for dripping taps:
Let your family know if you spot any dripping taps at home! These can waste considerable water and should be fixed promptly. They might also simply be taps that weren't turned off properly – make sure to check after every usage!

Make every drop count!

01
02
03
04

WATER EFFICIENCY

Water consumption:
Type of product:
Brand:
Model:

A
B

03. Use water-efficient appliances:
Do you see these water efficiency labels on your washing machine or toilet at home? Ask your family about them and encourage them to purchase products with higher efficiency. These may cost more to buy, but they help bring down the water bill in the long run, while helping to save the environment –a win–win situation!

04. Cooking and eating:
If you are rinsing many fruits or vegetables at the same time, try to rinse them in a container rather than under running water.

A. The more ticks on the water label, the more water-efficient the product!

B. The label also tells you how much water is consumed each time the product is run.

Different countries and regions have different water efficiency labels. Do you know what the label looks like in your area?

HOW CAN I INVOLVE OTHERS?

Here's how you can encourage those around you to learn more about water conservation and practise it:

Look out for local enrichment activities: Encourage your friends and family to join you in participating in young scientist or water ambassador programmes organised by your local science centre/ museum or water agency, and learn more about water conservation together.

Participate in World Water Day: Find out more about local initiatives to mark World Water Day, and help to raise awareness about them.

Join a club or write in: Look out for clubs or societies in your school relating to water conservation or sustainability, or create one on your own if it doesn't exist! Help to spread awareness of the issue by organising activities and writing to your school's magazine or local newspaper.

 Can you think of more ways to help and to spread the word?

Published by

WS Education, an imprint of
World Scientific Publishing Co. Pte. Ltd.
5 Toh Tuck Link, Singapore 596224
USA office: 27 Warren Street, Suite 401–402, Hackensack, NJ 07601
UK office: 57 Shelton Street, Covent Garden, London WC2H 9HE

National Library Board, Singapore Cataloguing in Publication Data
Name(s): Chan, Ronald, author. | Yee Wearn, illustrator.
Title: I can change the world ... with the turn of a tap / written by Ronald Chan ; illustrated by Yeewearn.
Other Title(s): I'm a scientist! (WS Education (Firm))
Description: Singapore : WS Education , [2022]
Identifier(s): ISBN 978-981-12-5747-6 (hardback) | 978-981-12-5748-3 (paperback) |
    978-981-12-5749-0 (ebook for institutions) | 978-981-12-5750-6 (ebook for individuals)
Subject(s): LCSH: Water conservation--Juvenile fiction. | Sustainable living--Juvenile fiction.
Classification: DDC 428.6--dc23

British Library Cataloguing-in-Publication Data
A catalogue record for this book is available from the British Library.

Copyright © 2022 by World Scientific Publishing Co. Pte. Ltd.
All rights reserved. This book, or parts thereof, may not be reproduced in any form or by any means, electronic or mechanical, including photocopying, recording or any information storage and retrieval system now known or to be invented, without written permission from the publisher.

For photocopying of material in this volume, please pay a copying fee through the Copyright Clearance Center, Inc., 222 Rosewood Drive, Danvers, MA 01923, USA. In this case permission to photocopy is not required from the publisher.

For any available supplementary material, please visit
https://www.worldscientific.com/worldscibooks/10.1142/12879#t=suppl

Printed in Singapore

To receive updates about children's titles from WS Education, go to https://www.worldscientific.com/page/newsletter/subscribe, choose "Education", click on "Children's Books" and key in your email address.

Follow us @worldscientificedu on Instagram and @World Scientific Education on YouTube for our latest releases, videos and promotions.

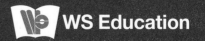